THE LITTLE BOOK OF

WHISKEY

TOM HAY

summersdale

THE LITTLE BOOK OF WHISKEY

An Hachette UK Company
www.hachette.co.uk

Summersdale Publishers Ltd
Part of Octopus Publishing Group Limited
Carmelite House
50 Victoria Embankment
LONDON
EC4Y 0DZ
UK

www.summersdale.com

Printed and bound in China

ISBN: 978-1-78685-796-5

Substantial discounts on bulk quantities of Summersdale books are available to corporations, professional associations and other organisations. For details contact general enquiries: telephone: +44 (0) 1243 771107 or email: enquiries@summersdale.com.

TO..

FROM..

THE WONDERFUL WORLD OF WHISKEY

Ah, whiskey. One of the most popular, varied and beguiling of all alcoholic beverages, whiskey is produced and enjoyed all around the world. From the smoky strength of a single-malt Scotch to the warming delights of an Irish coffee, and from spicy American rye whiskey to smooth and refined Japanese offerings, there's a world of whiskies at your fingertips – and this book is here to help you celebrate them all in style. Let's start with a quick history of our favourite spirit...

The practice of distilling spirits such as brandy, gin and vodka developed in the Middle Ages, and what we know as whiskey is believed to have emerged between the eleventh and thirteenth centuries, when Scottish and Irish monks substituted grain mash for the traditional grapes used to make alcohol. In the sixteenth century, following the dissolution of the monasteries in Britain, monks relied on distilling to make their living in the outside world, which made whiskey more widely available and popular than ever. But the imposition of taxes in the 1700s led to riots and heavily impacted whiskey production in Scotland, resulting in the illegal manufacture and smuggling of 'moonshine' – whiskey made and transported under the cover of darkness.

Meanwhile, European colonists had taken the distillation method with them to America in the seventeenth century, where new types of grain and mash were used to create variations on the traditional Scottish and Irish spirits – whiskey was even used as currency in the American War of Independence. The USA's own 'whiskey tax' in the 1790s, as well as Prohibition between 1920 and 1933, threatened to curtail American whiskey production, but by 1964 bourbon whiskey was popular enough to be declared a 'distinctive product of the United States'.

Today, though the Big Three (Scotland, Ireland and America) continue to be the biggest producers of whiskey – it is estimated that 34 bottles of Scotch are exported from Scotland every second, and Kentucky contains more barrels of bourbon than people – other countries such as Canada, Japan and Australia have thrown their hats into the ring to compete for the honour of making the world's finest whiskey.

HOW IS WHISKEY MADE?

Whiskey is a distilled spirit (just like vodka, gin and rum) made from grains, but what does that mean? Here's how humble grains are transformed into delicious whiskey, in five simple steps:

Malting: a process that forces the chosen grain (usually barley, rye, wheat or corn) to germinate – either on the malting floor or in a malting drum. The germination process is then stopped by drying out the grains (now called malt). They are then ground into a coarse flour called grist.

Mashing: hot water is added to the ground-down malt to create a mash. This porridge-like mixture is stirred  continuously in a mash tun to extract the malt sugar from the grist. The sugar water, known as wort, is then pumped out, leaving the husks behind.

Fermentation: yeast is added to the wort to convert the sugar into alcohol. At this stage of production, whiskey is essentially the same as beer.

Distillation: the liquid is purified, and water is removed to increase the proportion of alcohol by volume (ABV). The process traditionally takes place in large copper devices known as stills (nowadays they tend to be made of stainless steel, but lined with copper); pot stills are the most common, except in America where they prefer column stills.

Ageing: the distilled spirit is stored in wooden casks to mature – whiskey becomes smoother and more complex as it ages, and gains character and colour from the cask it is aged in.

WHISKY OR WHISKEY?

If you're new to the wonderful world of whiskey, here's a quick primer on the terminology you should know – but when in doubt, remember: all whiskey is good whiskey.

WHISKY

The word 'whisky' is derived from the Gaelic for 'water of life', *uisge beatha*. It refers to a distilled spirit made from fermented grain mash – various grains such as rye, barley, wheat or corn can be used, each providing a unique flavour profile. Most whiskies are aged in wooden barrels (casks), usually oak, for several years. Whiskies are produced all over the world.

WHISKEY

That little 'e' causes much confusion to those who aren't au fait with whiskey lingo, but really it's just a simple spelling variation that arose as whiskies travelled the world. Here's a simple way to remember which whiskies use this bonus-vowelled version: both of the countries that use this spelling have an 'e' in them (America and Ireland) while the other main whiskey producers don't (Scotland, Canada, Japan).

SCOTCH

To qualify as an official 'Scotch' whiskey, it needs to be produced and matured in Scotland, must be matured in oak for at least three years, and must be made from 100 per cent malted barley. Most barley is dried using peat, which gives Scotch its unique smoky flavour. There are over 80 whiskey distilleries in Scotland.

BOURBON

An American whiskey produced primarily in Kentucky, and made from at least 51 per cent corn. There is no age specification for bourbon, but 'straight' bourbons are aged for at least two years. They generally have a sweeter, smoother flavour than Scotch whiskies, with hints of caramel or vanilla.

RYE WHISKEY

Whiskey made with at least 51 per cent rye and matured for at least two years. Traditionally made in America but also widely produced in Canada, this whiskey has a spicier flavour than most others.

IRISH WHISKEY

Irish whiskies must include malted barley, but may be blended with other grains to create a wide variety of flavours. The only additives allowed are water and caramel colouring. The barley is not usually dried using peat, so Irish whiskies have a smoother, sweeter taste than Scotches.

MALT WHISKEY

'Malting' is the process by which barley is germinated to turn the starch into natural sugars, which are then fermented to create alcohol. Malted barley is traditionally twice-distilled in pot stills and then matured in oak for at least three years. In America, 'malted rye' refers to rye whiskey that has undergone the same malting process.

SINGLE CASK

The product of a single distillation run, these whiskies are bottled from a single cask, as opposed to being blended with whiskies from other casks or distilleries.

SINGLE MALT

A single malt is a malted whiskey produced from a single distillery, as opposed to being blended with whiskies from other distilleries. Single malt Scotch must be aged for at least three years.

BLENDED WHISKEY

A whiskey created by mixing the product of more than one distillation run or distillery. Producers will often mix a high-quality single malt with a cheaper whiskey (or sometimes another neutral grain spirit), and sometimes with extra colourings or flavourings, to create a more affordable spirit.

A WORLD OF FLAVOURS

Lots of different things affect the taste of each individual whiskey, and not just the ingredients – how the grains are dried, how long the whiskey is distilled for, how it's aged and how you drink it. Let's take a quick look at the main factors:

GRAINS

Barley tends to produce a whiskey with strong cereal flavours. Corn tends to produce sweeter, more vanilla- or syrupy-flavoured whiskies. Rye tends to produce spicy, peppery flavours. Wheat tastes... well, wheaty. Millet, oat, quinoa and other grains are also sometimes used and each offers their own distinct flavour profile.

WATER

The water used in the production of whiskey can have a great impact on its overall flavour. Many distilleries are built near to fresh springs so they can use the best-quality water to enhance the flavour of their whiskies.

PEAT

The use of peat in the malting process adds the distinctive 'smoky' flavour commonly associated with Scotch.

FERMENTATION

Increasing the length of time the yeast is left to react with the wort (the sugary liquid extracted from the mash) increases the complexity of flavours in the finished product.

DISTILLATION

The more times a whiskey is distilled, the more congeners (the flavours added to the liquid by the yeast) and impurities are removed. As these flavours tend to be harsher, a triple-distilled whiskey is usually smoother and lighter than a double-distilled one. The extra distillation can also make the spirit stronger and less aromatic.

AGEING

Whiskey is traditionally aged in oak casks, but the flavour of the final product varies greatly depending on whether producers use new oak or charred oak (which gives Bourbon its distinctive caramel and vanilla flavours), or if the casks have previously contained other alcohols, such as sherry or bourbon. The longer a whiskey is left to age, the more any sulphur compounds and volatile alcohols are sapped from it, and the more rounded the flavour becomes.

HOW IT'S SERVED

Most whiskey connoisseurs would argue that drinking whiskey neat allows you to appreciate the complexities of the spirit. But others claim that adding a (very small!) splash of water can open up the whiskey and release more of the aromas and subtle flavours, taking any harsh edges off and counteracting the numbing effect of the alcohol. If you opt for a whiskey on the rocks, make sure you use large ice cubes, to minimise dilution as they melt, or go with whiskey stones – stone cubes that will cool your drink without altering the flavour. In Spain whiskey is traditionally drunk with cola, and in China it is customary to drink whiskey with cold green tea!

HOW YOU TASTE IT

Whichever whiskey you go for, and however you like to drink it, be sure to 'nose' it first – swirl the liquid in the glass to release the aromas and then lift it to your nose to take in all the different scents. Then, when you take your first sip, notice the flavours that hit your tongue first, how it tastes in your mouth, and the finish it leaves behind. Enjoy!

WHAT YOU'LL NEED

Here is a list of essential items you will need when making the whiskey cocktails in this book:

- Cocktail glasses (most cocktails can be served in a traditional cocktail glass, an Old-Fashioned or rocks tumbler, or a highball glass, but some recipes call for a specific glass)
- Cocktail shaker (the Boston style is the most popular)
- Bar spoon
- Jigger and measuring spoons
- Muddler (a flat-bottomed instrument, similar to a pestle, used to bruise or mash cocktail ingredients)
- Lemon/lime squeezer
- Fine strainer
- Ice bucket
- Punch bowl/jug
- Ice
- Sugar syrup

OLD FASHIONED

The Old Fashioned was originally called 'the whiskey cocktail' and was supped in the morning to start the day with a kick. Its name was changed to distinguish it from the new generation of cocktails that were being invented in the 1870s, in recognition that this was the classic version.

INGREDIENTS

- 1 sugar cube or ½ tsp of caster sugar
- 3 dashes of aromatic bitters
- Dash of carbonated water (optional)
- 60 ml whiskey (rye or bourbon)

METHOD

Put the sugar into an Old-Fashioned glass.

Add the aromatic bitters; if you're new to this repertoire of flavours, stick to Angostura bitters, but if you'd like to be adventurous there are lots of others on the market for you to experiment with.

Add a dash of carbonated water (optional). Muddle (crush) the sugar while rotating the glass at an angle, so that the sugar grains and bitters create a lining.

Add ice. Finally, pour in the whiskey of your choice.

SALTED CARAMEL WHISKEY TRUFFLES

MAKES ABOUT 24 TRUFFLES

Rich cream, salted caramel and the bite of your favourite Irish whiskey, all wrapped up in one heavenly chocolatey cocoon – yum.

INGREDIENTS

- 100 g sugar
- 2 tbsp water
- 2 tbsp unsalted butter
- 1 tsp salt
- 230 ml double cream
- 300 g dark chocolate
- 180 ml Irish whiskey
- 70 g cocoa powder

METHOD

Heat the sugar and water in a saucepan, stirring frequently. Once the sugar has dissolved, increase heat to high and keep the mixture moving so that crystals do not form against the sides. When the mixture has darkened, add the butter, salt and 5 tbsp of cream and remove from the heat. Whisk the mixture to combine.

Meanwhile, melt the chocolate and remaining cream in a bowl placed over simmering water. Whisk until combined.

Remove the bowl from the heat and let it cool, then stir in the caramel sauce from the saucepan and the whiskey. Pour the resulting mix into a flat pan or tray, covering the surface with cling film, and refrigerate.

Once the mixture has set (around 3 hours), remove the mixture and scoop it into individual chocolate truffles. Form them by hand and place on a lined baking sheet.

Finally, dust the truffles with cocoa powder.

The worst thing
about some men
is that when they
are not drunk
they are sober.

W. B. YEATS

THE WATER WAS
NOT FIT TO DRINK. TO
MAKE IT PALATABLE, WE
HAD TO ADD WHISKEY.
BY DILIGENT EFFORT,
I LEARNED TO LIKE IT.

WINSTON CHURCHILL

I SHOULD NEVER HAVE SWITCHED FROM SCOTCH TO MARTINIS.

NICOLAS FREELING

MANHATTAN

This classic whiskey and vermouth cocktail hails from late nineteenth-century New York. For a traditional Manhattan, choose a rye whiskey; bourbon is an acceptable substitute but you'll lose some of that spicy edge.

INGREDIENTS

- 75 ml rye whiskey
- 30 ml sweet vermouth
- 2 dashes aromatic bitters
- 1 maraschino cherry

METHOD

Pour the whiskey, vermouth and bitters into an ice-filled shaker. Stir lightly and carefully, but well (shaking would make the cocktail cloudy to the eye and oily to the taste). Strain the drink into a cocktail glass and garnish with the cherry.

Whiskey
is liquid
sunshine.

GEORGE BERNARD SHAW

WHAT WHISKEY
WILL NOT CURE,
THERE IS NO
CURE FOR.

IRISH PROVERB

BOURBON GLAZE

This flavoursome glaze can be used to baste chicken, steak, ribs, tofu... Actually, it goes almost without saying that this will go on just about anything.

INGREDIENTS

- 250 ml bourbon whiskey
- 100 g brown sugar
- 6 tbsp ketchup
- 2 tbsp Worcestershire sauce
- 60 ml cider vinegar
- 1 pinch dry mustard
- Salt and pepper to taste

METHOD

Combine all of the ingredients in a bowl, adding the salt and pepper last to judge the taste. If not using immediately, store covered in the fridge and use within 24 hours.

*Reality is an
illusion created by
a lack of alcohol.*

N. F. SIMPSON

THE GREEN GIMLET

This variant of the traditional gimlet is known for its bright green appearance.

INGREDIENTS

- 4 basil leaves
- 15 ml lime juice
- 50 ml Scotch
- 15 ml sugar syrup
- Slice of lime or sprig of mint to garnish

METHOD

Muddle the basil leaves in a cocktail shaker, then add the lime juice. Fill the shaker with ice, then add the Scotch and the syrup and shake. Strain into a chilled cocktail glass and garnish with a slice of lime or a sprig of mint.

MY GRANDMOTHER
IS OVER 80 AND
STILL DOESN'T
NEED GLASSES.
DRINKS RIGHT OUT
OF THE BOTTLE.

HENNY YOUNGMAN

SLEEP LATE,
HAVE FUN,
GET WILD,
DRINK WHISKEY.

HUNTER S. THOMPSON

MINT JULEP

A 'julep' is generally considered to be a sweet drink. This particular cocktail originated in the US state of Kentucky.

INGREDIENTS

- 15 ml sugar syrup
- 4 mint leaves
- 60 ml bourbon whiskey

METHOD

Muddle the syrup and mint leaves in a highball glass. Add the bourbon and fill with crushed ice. Stir well until the glass is frosty. Garnish with any leftover mint.

Keep your friends close, but a bottle of whiskey closer.

EARL DIBBLES JR

Keep calm
AND DRINK
WHISKEY.

WHISKEY CREAM

A simple recipe that can be served alongside desserts of your choice. A particular treat at Christmas.

INGREDIENTS

- 250 ml double cream
- 30 ml whiskey of your choice – although Irish and bourbon whiskeys are particularly good
- 1 dessertspoon caster or icing sugar

METHOD

Whip the cream until it holds its shape, then gently stir in the whiskey and sugar.

I DRINK EXACTLY AS MUCH AS I WANT, AND ONE DRINK MORE.

H. L. MENCKEN

WHISKEY
AND ICE AND
EVERYTHING
NICE.

WHISKEY SMASH

The citrus-flavoured cocktail hails from the nineteenth century, but this recipe includes muddled lemon as a nod to the version created by 'King Cocktail' Dale DeGroff at the Rainbow Room in New York.

INGREDIENTS

- 2 slices lemon
- A handful of fresh mint leaves
- 60 ml bourbon whiskey
- 25 ml lemon juice
- 15 ml sugar syrup
- 1 mint sprig

METHOD

Muddle the lemon slices and mint leaves in the bottom of an Old-Fashioned glass and top with ice. Shake the bourbon, lemon juice and sugar syrup in a shaker with ice. Strain into the glass and garnish with the mint sprig.

Love makes the world go round? Not at all. Whiskey makes it go round twice as fast.

COMPTON MACKENZIE

Drink

HAPPY
THOUGHTS.

SCOTCH ROYALE

Adjust the amount of champagne to taste in this Prohibition-era cocktail – a 1:1 ratio leaves a lovely crisp taste, while more champagne will naturally result in a sweeter drink.

INGREDIENTS

- 1 sugar cube
- 40 ml Scotch whiskey
- 40–80 ml champagne
- 1 dash bitters

METHOD

Place the sugar cube in a champagne flute. Add the bitters and then the whiskey. Top up with the champagne.

HERE'S TO
ALCOHOL, THE
ROSE-COLOURED
GLASSES OF LIFE.

F. SCOTT FITZGERALD

BUT
FIRST,
WHISKEY.

WHISKEY-INFUSED FRUIT CAKE

SERVES 8

A fun variation on a traditional fruit cake, with whiskey baked into the mix to give it a rich taste. Perfect for Christmas and special occasions.

INGREDIENTS

- 300 g mixed dried fruit
- 70 g cherries, pitted and halved
- 400 ml orange juice
- 195 ml blended Scotch whiskey
- 190 g butter, diced
- 250 g brown sugar
- 2 large eggs
- 470 g plain flour
- 3 tsp baking powder

METHOD

Preheat the oven to 170°C.

Place the dried fruit, cherries, orange juice and half of the whiskey in a large saucepan. Bring this mixture to boil, then reduce to let it simmer for 5 minutes.

Turn off the heat and stir in the butter. Once the mixture has cooled somewhat, add the brown sugar, the remaining whiskey and the eggs and beat until smooth.

Sieve in the flour and baking powder at this point. Tip the batter into a greased tin and bake for one hour.

Once cooked, leave the cake to cool.

I drink to make other people more interesting.

ERNEST HEMINGWAY

ADVENTURES RUN ON ALL SORTS OF WHISKEY.

ATTICUS

BOURBON PUNCH

SERVES 8

The beauty of a punch is that you can chuck just about anything in there and be left with a big bowl of delicious fruity alcohol. Feel free to sub in other fruit juices, or even fruity iced teas.

INGREDIENTS

- 150 ml sugar syrup
- 250 ml orange juice
- 250 ml grapefruit juice
- 200 ml bourbon whiskey
- 150 ml water
- 125 ml lemon juice
- Orange and lemon slices, to garnish

METHOD

Combine all ingredients in a large bowl or pitcher and stir well. Add the fruit slices. Serve the punch over ice.

Alcohol may be
man's worst enemy,
but the Bible says
love your enemy.

FRANK SINATRA

SIP,
SIP,
HOORAY.

SAZERAC

Created by Antoine Peychaud in New Orleans in 1838, the Sazerac is often referred to as 'America's first cocktail'.

INGREDIENTS

- 1 sugar cube
- 3 dashes Peychaud's Bitters
- 35 ml rye whiskey
- 40 ml absinthe
- Lemon peel

METHOD

Fill one Old-Fashioned glass with ice. Place the sugar cube into a second Old-Fashioned glass and add the bitters to it. Muddle the sugar cube, then add the whiskey and stir. Dipose of the ice from the first glass and swirl the absinthe around it to coat the glass. Empty the contents of the second glass into the first and garnish with the lemon peel.

A MAN'S GOT
TO BELIEVE IN
SOMETHING.
I BELIEVE I'LL HAVE
ANOTHER DRINK.

W. C. FIELDS

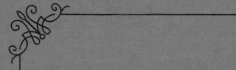

I'M ON A WHISKEY DIET. LAST WEEK I LOST THREE DAYS.

TOMMY COOPER

WHISKEY FUDGE

MAKES ABOUT 24 PIECES

A spectacular combination, containing both the crumbly, melt-in-your-mouth fudgey texture and the glorious taste of whiskey. Be very careful while making this recipe, as it gets very hot.

INGREDIENTS

- 600 ml double cream
- 350 g caster sugar
- 350 g brown sugar
- 100 g unsalted butter, plus extra for greasing
- 50 ml whiskey – Jack Daniel's works particularly well
- 50 g cocoa powder
- Pinch of salt

METHOD

Grease a deep baking tray or line with greaseproof paper.

Warm the cream, sugar and butter over a low heat, stirring continuously, until the sugar has dissolved.

If you have a sugar thermometer, attach it to your pan now. Increase the heat until the mixture comes to a rolling boil, or until it reaches 115°C, then reduce to a simmer for 2–3 minutes, stirring constantly to avoid burning.

Remove the pan from the heat and allow the mixture to cool to 110°C, and then add in the whiskey, cocoa powder and salt – be careful, as the mixture may bubble up.

Beat the mixture until it starts to lose its gloss, then pour into the prepared tray. Set aside to cool at room temperature.

Once it has cooled and firmed up, remove the fudge from the tin and cut into cubes with a sharp knife. Store in the fridge for up to three weeks.

There is no bad whiskey. There are only some whiskeys that aren't as good as others.

RAYMOND CHANDLER

Whiskey making is
an act of cooperation
between the blessings
of nature and the
wisdom of man.

MASATAKA TAKETSURU

LORD, GIVE ME
COFFEE TO CHANGE
THE THINGS I CAN,
AND WHISKEY
TO ACCEPT THE
THINGS I CAN'T.

ANONYMOUS

JOHN COLLINS

A variant of the Tom Collins, this sour cocktail traces its origins to the nineteenth century.

INGREDIENTS

- 60 ml bourbon whiskey
- 25 ml lemon juice
- 15 ml sugar syrup
- 3 dashes bitters
- Soda water
- Cocktail cherry
- 1 slice orange

METHOD

Shake the bourbon, lemon juice, sugar syrup and bitters together, then strain into a Collins glass. Top with soda water. Garnish with the cherry and orange.

THE CHURCHILL

The Churchill was created by Joe Gilmore, head barman at the London Savoy's American Bar, during one of Winston Churchill's many visits to the hotel.

INGREDIENTS

- 45 ml Scotch whiskey
- 15 ml lime juice
- 15 ml sweet vermouth
- 15 ml orange liqueur

METHOD

Mix ingredients with ice before straining into a chilled cocktail glass.

I have taken more
out of alcohol
than alcohol has
taken out of me.

WINSTON CHURCHILL

Save water.

DRINK
WHISKEY.

BUT I'M NOT SO
THINK AS YOU
DRUNK I AM.

J. C. SQUIRE

CRANACHAN

SERVES 4

An old Scottish dessert that was originally served in June, the harvest-time of raspberries.

INGREDIENTS

- 85 g porridge oats
- 450 g raspberries
- 570 ml double cream
- 75 ml Scotch whiskey
- 3 tbsp honey

METHOD

Toast the oats in a frying pan until they are browned but not burnt. Keeping several raspberries to one side, blend the rest into a puree. In a mixing bowl, whip the cream and the whiskey together and add in the honey. In individual serving glasses, layer the dessert with the cream and raspberry puree at the bottom, then the oats, then more cream and finally some whole raspberries to top it off.

NEVER DELAY KISSING A PRETTY GIRL OR OPENING A BOTTLE OF WHISKEY.

ERNEST HEMINGWAY

THAT PERFECT MOMENT WHEN IT'S TOO LATE FOR COFFEE BUT TOO EARLY FOR SCOTCH: TIME FOR IRISH COFFEE.

IRISH COFFEE

The Irish coffee is said to have been invented by Joe Sheridan on a cold night in 1942, in an airbase in the west of Ireland, to warm passengers.

INGREDIENTS

- 1 cup of coffee (freshly roasted if possible, but filter will do)
- 1 tsp sugar
- 1 tsp brown sugar
- 45 ml Irish whiskey
- 30 ml cold double cream, lightly whipped

METHOD

Fill a heat-proof glass with hot water and leave for 5–10 minutes to warm, then empty the hot water from the glass. Fill with coffee, then pour in the whiskey and sugars and stir. Top with an inch of cream, poured over the back of a spoon.

You're not drunk
if you can lie on
the floor without
holding on.

DEAN MARTIN

I wish to live to 150 years old, but the day I die, I wish it to be with a cigarette in one hand and a glass of whiskey in the other.

AVA GARDNER

RUSTY NAIL

The Rusty Nail was the drink of choice of the Rat Pack during the 1960s. Order one of these on a night out for instant Sinatra vibes.

INGREDIENTS

- 50 ml Scotch whiskey
- 25 ml Drambuie liqueur
- Lemon twist, to garnish

METHOD

Pour the ingredients into an ice-filled Old-Fashioned glass and stir gently. Garnish with lemon.

My god, so much I like to drink Scotch that sometimes I think my name is Igor Stra-whiskey.

IGOR STRAVINSKY

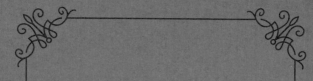

Whiskey... the oil of conversation, the philosophic wine, the ale that is consumed when good fellows get together, that puts a song in their hearts and laughter on their lips, and the warm glow of contentment in their eyes.

NOAH SWEAT

WHISKEY MUSTARD

A classic sauce given a whiskey twist. The choice of whiskey will affect the overall flavour, so if you prefer something tangy, try a spicy Scotch; for a sweeter taste, go for a warm Irish whiskey.

INGREDIENTS

- 60 g yellow mustard seeds
- 60 g brown mustard seeds
- 250 ml white wine vinegar
- 100 ml water
- 75 ml whiskey of your choice
- 100 g brown sugar
- 1 tsp salt

METHOD

Coarsely grind the mustard seeds, then place them in a bowl with the vinegar, water and whiskey and cover with a tea towel. Leave at room temperature for two days. Place in a blender with the brown sugar and salt and blend until smooth. Decant into a sterilised jar and store in the fridge for up to three weeks.

HAVING A
FULL BOTTLE
IN FRONT
OF ME IS A
SERIOUSLY
WHISKEY
BUSINESS.

WHISKEY IS SIMPLY
SUNSHINE HELD
TOGETHER BY WATER.

ANONYMOUS

AMBER MOON

This cocktail is an acquired taste, and is believed to help cure hangovers. It's also the 'breakfast' of choice of the unfortunate victim in *Murder on the Orient Express*, but don't let that put you off!

INGREDIENTS

- 1 raw egg
- 75 ml whiskey
- 1 dash Tabasco sauce

METHOD

Crack the egg into a highball glass, taking care to leave the yolk intact. Pour in the whiskey and add the Tabasco.

Always carry a flagon of whiskey in case of a snake bite and, furthermore, always carry a small snake.

W. C. FIELDS

Whiskey:

BECAUSE NO GREAT STORY EVER STARTED WITH WATER.

FOUR HORSEMEN

Jack, Jim, Johnnie and Jameson – four famous men, four great whiskies, one potent hit.

INGREDIENTS

- 15 ml Jack Daniel's whiskey
- 15 ml Jim Beam bourbon
- 15 ml Johnnie Walker Scotch
- 15 ml Jameson Irish whiskey

METHOD

Pour all four ingredients into an Old-Fashioned glass and serve.

It is true that whiskey improves with age. The older I get, the more I like it.

RONNIE CORBETT

Whiskey has killed more men than bullets, but most men would rather be full of whiskey than bullets.

LOGAN PEARSALL SMITH

CHOCOLATE WHISKEY MOUSSE

SERVES 2

Light, creamy, and now – alcoholic! This tasty dessert will make a fine finale to any meal.

INGREDIENTS

- 2 large eggs
- 150 g milk chocolate, broken into small pieces
- 30 g butter
- 1 tbsp instant coffee granules
- 30 ml Scotch whiskey
- 60 g sugar
- Pinch salt
- 120 ml double cream

METHOD

Separate the egg yolks and whites.

Place the chocolate, butter and coffee in a bowl placed over a saucepan of simmering water to melt. Once the butter has melted, take it off the heat and stir in the whiskey.

In a separate bowl, whisk the egg yolks and all but 2 tbsp of sugar in a bowl placed over a saucepan of simmering water until the mixture becomes foamy, then add to the chocolate mix.

Beat the egg whites with a pinch of salt, and then gradually add in 2 tbsp of sugar. Add to the previous mix.

Beat the double cream well, then add to the mix.

Give the mixture one final thorough stir and then divide into two serving glasses and refrigerate for up to 12 hours. Serve chilled.

HAPPINESS IS
HAVING A RARE STEAK,
A BOTTLE OF WHISKEY
AND A DOG TO EAT
THE RARE STEAK.

JOHNNY CARSON

ALL
WHISKEY
IS GOOD
WHISKEY.

THE RED AKUMA

This spicy Japanese cocktail has quite the kick — and lots of flavour.

INGREDIENTS

- 250 ml blood orange juice
- 2 tsp agave syrup
- 125 ml Japanese whiskey
- 1 jalapeño pepper, chopped

METHOD

Mix the juice, syrup and whiskey in a shaker and stir. Add the chopped jalapeño pepper and shake vigorously. Strain into an ice-filled Old-Fashioned glass.

I'm not a heavy drinker; I can sometimes go for hours without touching a drop.

NOËL COWARD

According to chemistry, **WHISKEY IS A SOLUTION.**

WHISKEY SOUR

This classic sweet-and-sour whiskey cocktail dates back to at least 1870, and its sharp, sophisticated flavour has been a favourite ever since.

INGREDIENTS

- 1 tsp caster sugar
- 60 ml whiskey (rye or bourbon)
- 30 ml fresh lemon juice
- ½ egg white (optional)
- Maraschino cherry, to garnish
- Slice of orange peel, to garnish

METHOD

Dissolve the sugar in the whiskey by stirring in a shaker mixed with ice. Then add the lemon juice and egg white (optional) and shake vigorously. If adding egg white, make sure you shake the mixture at least a minute longer in order to create a thick texture. Serve in a cocktail glass and garnish with a cherry and a slice of orange peel held over a flame for a couple of seconds.

COURAGE IS A VITAMIN BEST SWALLOWED WITH WHISKEY.

JAROD KINTZ

I'm a drinker with
a writing problem.

BRENDAN BEHAN

WHISKEY-CURED JERKY

MAKES 5 SERVINGS

Jerky is sometimes regarded as being bland and chewy, but this recipe will change your mind. Add some flavour to the snack with your own choice of whiskey.

INGREDIENTS

- 125 ml whiskey
- 100 g brown sugar
- 125 ml soy sauce
- 125 ml cider vinegar
- 1 tbsp Worcestershire sauce
- 4 drops liquid hickory smoke
- 500 g cooked jerky strips

METHOD

Place all ingredients apart from the meat in a sealable freezer bag and thoroughly mix. Leave to rest for 10 minutes, then add the cooked meat.

Mix the meat around so that it absorbs the marinade, then place the bag in the fridge for 24 hours.

When the marinade has properly soaked into the meat, remove the strips and leave to dry.

Store in a sealed container at room temperature for up to a month.

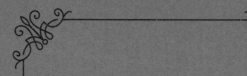

My own experience has been that the tools I need for my trade are paper, tobacco, food, and a little whiskey.

WILLIAM FAULKNER

TORONTO

Canadian whiskey – traditionally lighter and more mellow than its American counterparts – is perfectly complemented here by the complex herbal flavours of Fernet Branca. If you've never tried Fernet before, you might want to increase the amount of sugar syrup slightly to tame its bitter bite.

INGREDIENTS

- 60 ml Canadian whiskey
- 1½ tsp Fernet Branca liqueur
- 1½ tsp sugar syrup
- 1 dash Angostura bitters
- Orange slice, to garnish

METHOD

Stir all ingredients in an ice-filled shaker before straining into a chilled coupe glass. Garnish with the orange slice.

*I distrust camels,
and anyone else
who can go a week
without a drink.*

JOE E. LEWIS

WHISKEY MAC

The Whiskey MacDonald (to give it its full name) was created by Colonel Hector MacDonald during his time in India under the British Raj.

INGREDIENTS

- 45 ml blended Scotch
- 30 ml ginger wine

METHOD

Fill an Old-Fashioned glass with ice, then pour in the whiskey and ginger wine. Stir lightly.

I TAKE THE JUICE
OF TWO QUARTS
OF WHISKEY.

EDDIE CONDON
ON HIS HANGOVER CURE

I followed my heart and it led me to whiskey.

ANONYMOUS

WHISKEY CARAMEL

This thick, gooey sauce can be eaten with dessert, used in recipes that call for caramel, or eaten straight out of the pan.

INGREDIENTS

- 100 g butter
- 200 g brown sugar
- 60 ml bourbon whiskey
- ½ tsp salt
- 100 ml double cream

METHOD

Melt the butter in a saucepan, then add the sugar. Mix well, then add the whiskey and salt. Let the mix simmer for 5 minutes, stirring frequently. Add the cream and let the mixture simmer until it has thickened, stirring once every few minutes. Once cooled, transfer to a sterilised jar and store, refrigerated, for up to three weeks.

The earliest pioneer of civilisation... is never the steamboat, never the railroad... never the missionary — but always whiskey!

MARK TWAIN

Whiskey improves with age...

AND I IMPROVE WITH WHISKEY.

WARD 8

This cocktail, named after a district in Boston, was first served in the Locke-Ober cafe by Tom Hussion in November 1898.

INGREDIENTS

- 60 ml American rye whiskey
- 15 ml lemon juice
- 15 ml orange juice
- 1 tsp grenadine
- 2 maraschino cherries

METHOD

Pour the whiskey, lemon juice, orange juice and grenadine into a shaker with ice, then shake and strain into a chilled cocktail glass. Garnish with the cherries.

NOW IS THE TIME
FOR DRINKING,
NOW THE TIME TO
DANCE FOOTLOOSE
UPON THE EARTH.

HORACE

Sober or blotto,
this is your motto:
keep muddling
through.

P. G. WODEHOUSE

MISSOURI MULE

Created for President Harry S. Truman, the Missouri Mule commemorates his home state, where the mule is the official animal.

INGREDIENTS

- 50 ml bourbon whiskey
- 50 ml applejack or Calvados
- 50 ml lemon juice
- 25 ml Campari
- 25 ml orange liqueur

METHOD

Shake the ingredients with ice, then strain into a cocktail glass.

Drink because you are happy, but never because you are miserable.

G. K. CHESTERTON

IT'S BETTER TO BE ONE PERSON'S SHOT OF WHISKEY THAN EVERYBODY'S CUP OF TEA.

SCOTCH-GLAZED MUSHROOMS

SERVES 4

This rich, warm and smoky recipe makes a perfect side dish, or why not try stirring it through tagliatelle for a quick and delicious pasta dish?

INGREDIENTS

- 500 g mushrooms
- 2 tbsp butter or oil
- 2 cloves garlic, minced
- 60 ml Scotch whiskey
- Salt and pepper

METHOD

Chop the mushrooms and cook them with the oil or butter until they're sizzling. Add the garlic. After a minute, add the Scotch. Stir well until the Scotch has cooked off. Add salt and pepper, then serve warm.

Whiskey is by far the most popular of all the remedies that won't cure a cold.

JERRY VALE

Why limit
happy
**TO AN
HOUR?**

HONEY PEACH FIZZ

The perfect refreshing summer cocktail: fresh and fruity.

INGREDIENTS

- 45 ml Jack Daniel's Tennessee Honey
- 30 ml lemon-lime soda
- 3 slices ripe peach
- 4 mint leaves

METHOD

Muddle the peach slices and mint leaves in an Old-Fashioned glass. Fill the glass with ice. Add the honey whiskey and soda, then stir lightly. Garnish with mint or more peach.

It takes only one drink to get me drunk. The trouble is, I can't remember if it's the thirteenth or the fourteenth.

GEORGE BURNS

ABSTAINER: A WEAK
PERSON WHO YIELDS
TO THE TEMPTATION
OF DENYING HIMSELF
A PLEASURE.

AMBROSE BIERCE

LYNCHBURG LEMONADE

This cocktail was created by Alabama restaurant and lounge owner Tony Mason in 1980. It was named after Lynchburg, Tennessee, home of the Jack Daniel's distillery.

INGREDIENTS

- 45 ml Tennessee whiskey
- 30 ml orange liqueur
- 30 ml lemon juice
- Lemon-lime soda
- Slice of lemon

METHOD

Pour the whiskey, orange liqueur and lemon juice into a shaker with ice. Shake, then strain into an ice-filled Collins glass. Top up with the soda and garnish with a lemon slice.

*What's drinking?
A mere pause
from thinking!*

LORD BYRON

SCOTCH BUTTER

MAKES ENOUGH FOR 12 SERVINGS

Simple and straightforward, whiskey butter can substitute for butter in most recipes to give your baking an alcoholic twist, or you can serve it on hot bacon or sausages for a fry-up with a kick.

INGREDIENTS

- 100 g butter
- 15 ml Scotch whiskey

Optional extras:

- 1 tsp wholegrain mustard
- Pinch chilli powder, salt or black pepper
- 1 shallot, finely chopped and fried

METHOD

Beat the whiskey and any optional extras into the butter until blended together. Voilà!

The proper drinking of Scotch whiskey is more than indulgence: it is a toast to civilisation, a tribute to the continuity of culture, a manifesto of man's determination to use the resources of nature to refresh mind and body and enjoy to the full the senses with which he has been endowed.

DAVID DAICHES

**Alcohol is necessary
for a man so that
he can have a good
opinion of himself,
undisturbed
by the facts.**

FINLEY PETER DUNNE

HOT TODDY

An ancient Scottish recipe, the hot toddy is said to aid recovery from a cold or the flu – a good excuse for some whiskey if ever there was one.

INGREDIENTS

- 1 tsp honey
- 60 ml Scotch whiskey
- 15 ml lemon juice
- 15 ml sugar syrup
- 3 dried cloves
- Boiling water (enough to fill the glass)

METHOD

Place a teaspoon of honey in a heatproof glass or mug, then add the other ingredients in the order listed. Stir until the honey has completely dissolved, and scoop out the cloves just before drinking.

I DRINK MY WHISKEY
NEAT AND LIVE
MY LIFE MESSY.

MATT BAKER

MONEY CAN'T BUY
YOU HAPPINESS.
BUT IT CAN BUY
YOU WHISKEY,
AND THAT'S
PRETTY CLOSE.

SHANDY MAKER

A classic beer cocktail with a citrusy twist.

INGREDIENTS

- 1 sprig fresh marjoram
- 50 ml bourbon whiskey
- 20 ml grapefruit juice
- 1½ tsp lemon juice
- 1½ tsp sugar syrup
- 85 ml pale ale

METHOD

Muddle the marjoram in a shaker, then add all other ingredients except the beer. Shake lightly, then strain into a pint glass filled with ice. Top with the beer.

*Too much work
and no vacation,
Deserves at least
a small libation.*

OSCAR WILDE

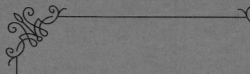

There is nothing which has yet been contrived by man, by which so much happiness is produced as by a good tavern or inn.

SAMUEL JOHNSON

WHISKEY MARMALADE

MAKES 3 JARS

A variation on Paddington's favourite snack, the oranges in this recipe can be easily switched for any other citrus fruit to make a sticky, delicious spread.

INGREDIENTS

- 1.5 kg oranges
- 2 litres water
- 40 ml lemon juice
- 2 kg sugar
- 2 tbsp treacle
- 125 ml Irish whiskey

METHOD

Put the whole, washed oranges and the water and lemon juice into a large pan (making sure the oranges are covered), and bring to the boil.

Leave simmering for 2½ hours, then remove from the heat and take out the oranges using a slotted spoon, retaining the cooking water.

When the oranges are cool enough to handle, scoop out the flesh from each orange (retain the peel) and return to the pan, and simmer for 30 minutes.

Strain the contents through a sieve, pressing as much pulp through as possible, then return to the pan.

Add the orange peel (sliced into thin strips), sugar and treacle, and bring back to the boil. Boil for 8–10 minutes, then pour in the whiskey and stir.

Remove the pan from the heat and allow to cool to room temperature. Store in sterilised jars for up to three months.

I DRINK WHEN I HAVE
OCCASION, AND
SOMETIMES WHEN I
HAVE NO OCCASION.

MIGUEL DE CERVANTES

This evening's forecast:

99% CHANCE OF WHISKEY.

WHISKEY ICED TEA

SERVES 10

Add a kick to your refreshing iced tea with these simple variations of tea, whiskey and fruit: black tea, bourbon and blackberries; green tea, Scotch and grapefruit; Earl Grey tea, Irish whiskey and peaches; black tea, rye whiskey and oranges.

INGREDIENTS

- 6 teabags
- 1 litre water
- 25 g sugar
- 25 ml lemon juice
- 100 ml whiskey of your choice
- 100 ml fruit juice or 250 g mashed fresh fruit of your choice
- 1 large handful of mint leaves

METHOD

Boil the water and steep the teabags in it with the sugar for 10 minutes, stirring occasionally, then remove the teabags and transfer the tea to a heatproof jug.

When it has cooled to room temperature, add the lemon juice, mint leaves, whiskey and fruit, and stir, leaving for at least 2 hours for the flavours to infuse.

Place in the fridge to chill for a few hours.

Serve in a highball or Old-Fashioned glass and garnish with extra mint leaves.

Health – what my friends are always drinking to before they fall down.

PHYLLIS DILLER

BOURBON SWIZZLE

A simple delight, made with ingredients you'll find in any well-stocked drinks cabinet.

INGREDIENTS

- 45 ml bourbon whiskey
- 30 ml lime juice
- 3 dashes bitters
- 60 ml soda water
- Wedge of lemon

METHOD

Fill a shaker with ice and add the bourbon, lime juice and bitters. Shake well, then strain into a highball glass half filled with ice. Add the soda water and garnish with a lemon wedge.

A GOOD GULP OF
HOT WHISKEY AT
BEDTIME – IT'S NOT
VERY SCIENTIFIC,
BUT IT HELPS.

ALEXANDER FLEMING

IT DOESN'T MATTER IF THE GLASS IS HALF FULL OR HALF EMPTY, AS LONG AS THERE'S WHISKEY IN IT.

SCOTCH WHISKEY SAUCE

SERVES 4

This Scottish sauce is traditionally consumed on Burns Night, served over haggis.

INGREDIENTS

- 30 ml Scotch whiskey
- 150 ml double cream
- 1 tbsp wholegrain mustard
- Salt and pepper

METHOD

Heat the whiskey in a saucepan over a high heat until it has cooked off. Add the double cream and mustard and stir. Lower the heat, add salt and pepper to season, and stir until the mixture has a thick consistency. Best used immediately.

Whiskey...
demands
appreciation.
You gaze first,
then it's time
to drink.

HARUKI MURAKAMI

SOUP OF
THE DAY:
WHISKEY,
WITH H_2O
CROUTONS.

PICKLEBACK

One of the more recent (and unusual) cocktails out there, the Pickleback uses the brine of gherkins to soothe after the bite of the whiskey.

INGREDIENTS

- 30 ml Irish whiskey
- 30 ml pickled gherkin brine

METHOD

Pour the whiskey into one shot glass and the brine into another. Drink the whiskey first, with the brine as a chaser.

Teetotallers lack the sympathy and generosity of men that drink.

W. H. DAVIES

SMILE.
THERE'S
WHISKEY.

BOURBON SLUSHIE

SERVES 2

This frozen cocktail needs to be made in advance, but when that hot weather strikes, you'll be glad you did!

INGREDIENTS

- 200 ml boiling water
- 2 black teabags
- 50 g sugar
- 250 ml orange juice
- 300 ml lemonade
- 100 ml bourbon whiskey
- 25 ml lime juice
- Soda water (optional)

METHOD

In a measuring jug, steep the teabags in the water for 10 minutes, then remove.

Dissolve the sugar in the tea and allow to cool. Add the orange juice, lemonade, bourbon and lime juice, and stir.

Pour into a freezable container, such as airtight freezer bags or a plastic container, and place in the freezer for at least 8 hours, or preferably overnight.

Remove from the freezer 10 minutes before you want to serve it. You can either use a masher to break up the frozen block, or scoop out chunks to put into serving glasses (either rocks or coupe glasses).

For a strong flavour, drink straight, but if you prefer a more refreshing treat, top up with soda water before serving.

There is a time and a place for a Scotch: **NOW AND IN MY HAND.**

APPLE AND CINNAMON WHISKEY

MAKES 1 LARGE JAR

Infusing your own flavours into whiskey is fairly simple and can enhance your favourite brand, or improve the taste of a not-so great whiskey.

INGREDIENTS

- 3 apples (not cooking apples)
- 2 cinnamon sticks
- 750 ml bourbon or Scotch whiskey
- 3 tbsp sugar

METHOD

Chop the apples into quarters or smaller slices, and place in a large, clean jar with the cinnamon sticks. Pour the whiskey over, and add the sugar. Seal the jar and leave to infuse, shaking every other day. The longer you leave it, the stronger the flavours will be, but around two weeks is recommended.

The problem with the world is that everyone is a few drinks behind.

HUMPHREY BOGART

MY DOCTOR TOLD
ME TO DRINK MORE
WATER. SO I ADDED
ANOTHER ICE CUBE
TO MY SCOTCH.

ALGONQUIN

Although the exact story of its creation is unknown, the Algonquin is known to have originated in the Algonquin Hotel in New York City in the 1930s.

INGREDIENTS

- 50 ml rye whiskey
- 25 ml vermouth
- 25 ml pineapple juice
- 1 dash bitters
- Orange peel or pineapple wedge, to garnish

METHOD

Stir the whiskey, vermouth, pineapple juice and bitters with ice, then strain into a chilled cocktail glass. Garnish with orange peel or a pineapple wedge.

**Keeping one's
guests supplied
with liquor is
the first law of
hospitality.**

MARGARET WAY

NO ANIMAL
EVER INVENTED
ANYTHING SO BAD
AS DRUNKENNESS
– OR SO GOOD
AS DRINK.

G. K. CHESTERTON

CROWNBERRY APPLE

The Crownberry Apple is one of the simplest cocktails you'll ever make, and a perfect introduction for those new to the world of whiskey.

INGREDIENTS

- 45 ml Crown Royal Regal Apple whiskey
- 120 ml cranberry juice
- Slice or wheel of apple

METHOD

Add the whiskey to a rocks glass filled with ice, then top with cranberry juice and stir. Garnish with a slice or wheel of apple.

*When I drink,
I think; and when
I think, I drink.*

FRANÇOIS RABELAIS

The light music
of whiskey falling
into glasses...
an agreeable
interlude.

JAMES JOYCE

BLUE CHEESE WHISKEY BURGER

SERVES 4

This modern recipe combines a sweet whiskey glaze with the mouth-watering taste of burgers packed with blue cheese.

INGREDIENTS

For the burgers:

- 600 g ground beef or meat-free mince
- 100 g blue cheese, cut into squares
- 1 onion, finely chopped
- Salt and pepper
- 4 burger buns

For the whiskey glaze:

- 60 ml Irish whiskey
- 3 tbsp ketchup
- 2 tbsp soy sauce
- 2 tbsp honey
- 1 tsp mustard
- 1 tsp Worcestershire sauce
- ¼ tsp pepper

METHOD

Mix the mince and onion together. Divide the mixture into four and shape them into patties, wrapping each around a square of blue cheese.

Season with salt and pepper and then grill until they are as done as you like.

For the glaze, combine all ingredients in a high-heat saucepan and cook until the mixture boils. Then lower heat to a simmer until the mixture thickens.

To serve, place the cooked burger patties in buns and drizzle the whiskey sauce over the top.

TOO MUCH OF
ANYTHING IS BAD,
BUT TOO MUCH
WHISKEY IS
BARELY ENOUGH.

MARK TWAIN

*All's well
that ends*

**WITH
WHISKEY.**

If you're interested in finding out more about our books, find us on Facebook at **Summersdale Publishers** and follow us on Twitter at **@Summersdale**.

www.summersdale.com

IMAGE CREDITS